Usborne
Write Your Own
Adventure
Stories

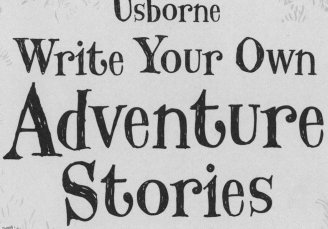

Usborne
Write Your Own
Adventure
Stories

Featuring chilling, teeth-grinding,
death-defying stories written by

Write your name here.

Contents

This section has lots of space for you to write your own stories in.

These pages have writing activities to get you started.

Story writing section

In a story about spies and espionage, who can you trust?

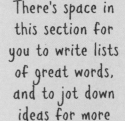

Stories don't always have to be completely made up.

Story writing toolkit

This section is full of tips and exercises to help you plan your stories and polish your writing skills.

There's space in this section for you to write lists of great words, and to jot down ideas for more stories.

Getting into the action

Adventure stories are filled with excitement, action and danger. They often start with a dramatic event that jolts the main character out of everyday life.

To get you started, here's an outline for a story. The opening lines have been written for you and there's space to write what happens next.

I woke up this morning with the smell of burning in my nostrils. Even with the curtains closed I could see blazing flames outside the window. So I...

What do you see when you open the curtains? How do you feel? What's your escape plan?

Story idea words

Scorching flames

Panic

Greasy smoke

Flashing lights

Trapped

Firefighters

However...

Your plan is thwarted. Perhaps smoke is seeping in under the door or someone is trapped in the next room.

How do you overcome the problem? Does anyone, or anything, come to help?

Then...

How does your story end? Do you escape? Is the fire put out? Perhaps a herd of elephants passes and they dowse the flames with water from their trunks.

Eventually...

Gushing water

ESCAPE

Coughing fit

Smashing glass

Rescue

Planning a story

It's a good idea to plan a story before you write it, to decide what you want to happen in each part. One way to do this is to imagine you're sending your hero on a journey over a lopsided mountain.

❸ Climax
This is the dramatic high point. Your hero encounters his or her greatest challenge, confronts an enemy or seems to face certain death.

❷ Build-up
Build up the tension and excitement. This part is full of action, twists and turns.

❹ Resolution
This is where you resolve any problems. Perhaps your hero escapes danger or defeats an enemy.

❶ Beginning
This is where you introduce your hero. Something happens to get the story started – maybe something frightening, mysterious or dangerous.

❺ End
Give your story a sad or happy ending.

Twists and turns

Adventure stories often involve an intriguing twist around the climax. Say your story is about a brilliant scientist. Mysterious agents kidnap her, but she manages to escape. That could be the climax – but if you add a twist, the agents could turn out to be something unexpected. For example, they could be...

allies trying to protect the scientist from something even more sinister...

or mutants from a failed experiment, who need her help to find a cure.

Your turn

Fill in this table to plan a story with an extra twist at the summit.
It could be about the kidnapped scientist – or anything else you like.

Title

Beginning

Build-up

Climax (with a twist)

Resolution

End

Creating a character

The best stories have characters that are intriguing and believable. Think about what makes your characters tick – if you really care about them, your reader will too.

Character ideas

You and your friends could star in your story.

Take someone from TV or a movie. To make things different you could imagine what that person was like as a child.

You could take a famous figure from history. Is your story set in his or her own time, or in the present day?

Your characters could be animals or even aliens.

Try inventing a character by filling out this questionnaire.

You could draw a picture of your character here.

Name...

What is he/she/it afraid of?

What is his/her/its greatest ambition?

What keeps him/her/it awake at night?

Who is his/her/its best friend?

Who does he/she/it most admire?

What word best describes him/her/it?

Too strong?

Give your characters weaknesses as well as strengths. It adds to the tension if there's a chance they might not succeed.

What would your character do?

Now imagine your character in a dangerous situation – perhaps on board a sinking ship. Use the space below to describe how your character reacts, thinks and feels. Does he or she try to help other people, or just save his or her own skin?

Standing out

Great characters often have distinctive traits. This makes them more memorable and easier for readers to picture.

Maybe your character has masses of curly hair...

or a limp or a wooden leg...

or a foreign accent...

or always wears dark glasses.

Show not tell

Telling people what to think makes writing boring. It's often better to show what's happening by describing a character's actions. Then readers can imagine it for themselves.

How to show

Here you can see how a couple of 'tells' can be turned into much more interesting 'shows'.

Tell: Joe was scared of heights.

Show: Joe looked down from the top of the skyscraper and immediately felt dizzy. His legs wobbled and he thought he was going to faint.

Tell: Jenny was beautiful.

Show: When Joe saw Jenny on the other side of the street he was so enchanted he walked into a lamppost.

Here are some **tells** for you to turn into **shows**. If you get stuck, there are some ideas on the right hand page.

Tell: Amy was brave.

Show:

Tell: Jack was frightened.

Show:

Tell: Sam was hungry.
Show:

Tell: The kayak was heavy.
Show:

Tell: The jungle was hot and humid.
Show:

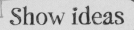

Show ideas

Protecting
a friend

Fending off a
hungry tiger

Heart
beating
hard

Goosebumps

Stomach gurgling

**Mouth
watering**

Can't stop
thinking
about food

EYES BULGING

Muscles straining

Buckling under
the weight

Sweat dripping

Wilting like
a flower

13

Start talking

When characters talk, this is called 'dialogue'. Using dialogue can be a more exciting way to move the action along than just describing what's happening.

Imagine you are out stargazing one night when you bump into an alien who tries to talk you into going into space with him.

Use the speech balloons on these pages to write a dialogue of what happens next.

You could use blue for your speech, and mauve for the alien, or vice versa.

Dialogue ideas

* Does the alien sound friendly or scary?

* Does he tell you who he is, where he comes from and where he is going?

* Is it a funny, friendly conversation – or an argument?

* Perhaps at first you misunderstand each other. Do you come to an agreement in the end?

Story
writing
section

Your stories

The following pages are packed with inspiring ideas and suggestions to help you write your own adventure stories. You can start writing right away, or you could turn to the 'Story Writing Toolkit' on pages 80-95 for more writing tips and checklists.

Write your story titles here as you go along.

18

24

28

32

36

40

46

52

56

61

66

70

74

78

Race to the summit

Two teams of mountaineers set out on a treacherous climb, racing to be the first humans ever to reach the top of Mount Peril. Will your hero get there first, or will his arch rival Dan Devious beat him to it?

These pages have suggestions to help with the different stages of your story as you go along.

Write your story title here.

Beginning

Introduce your hero and set the scene. What happens to get the story started? Does Dan Devious lay down a challenge? Is there a prize for the first to the top?

Heroes and villains

Most adventure stories have a hero and a villain – known as the 'protagonist' and the 'antagonist'.

The protagonist is the character everyone likes and wants to succeed. The antagonist is an enemy who is trying to thwart or destroy the protagonist.

Rivalry between a hero and a villain helps build tension in a story, and makes it more exciting to read.

Build-up

Build up the tension. What difficulties might prevent your hero from reaching the summit? Being caught in an avalanche? Taking a wrong turn? Does Dan Devious use any dirty tricks?

Dan Devious's dastardly character

Here are some ways you could **show not tell** what Dan Devious is like.

Dan likes to punch the air and say "Yessss!!!!"

He hates losing so much he even cheats playing chess with children.

His dad was the first man to climb Mount Everest with one hand tied behind his back. Dan has been trying to do something more impressive ever since.

Continued...

Who reaches the top first? Do they battle it out to claim the victory? What do they say to each other? Does Dan Devious reveal a secret that explains his motives?

→ Summit

Useful words

Resentment

Surly

Swagger

Avalanche

Bragging

JEALOUSY

Chilled to the bone

Icicles on nose

Nooks and crannies

Blown over by the wind

Sheltering in a cave

Bleak vista

Resolution

How do the climbers get back down? Are they still racing? Or do they have to work together? Do the rivals become friends?

End

What happens when they return home? Is there a celebration for the winner? Disgrace or punishment for the loser? Or does something really unexpected happen?

A spooky adventure

A brother and sister take a wrong turn on their way home. Suddenly they realize they're lost. There's something strange and unsettling about the place. Is it haunted or are they imagining things?

Locations

Ruins

Dark forest

Deserted house

Rundown hotel

Windy beach at dusk

Sense of place

Try to make your readers feel as if they are part of the adventure. The best way to do this is to use all five senses to give an atmospheric description of the setting.

How would you describe an abandoned old school using the five senses?

* What does it **smell** like? Musty and dusty?

* What do the walls feel like to **touch**? Damp? Clammy?

* Can you **hear** strange, distant sounds, like wailing souls? Or is it just the wind?

* What can you **see** at the window? Eerie shadows, flickering lights?

* Does the air **taste** cold on your tongue? And is it sour, too?

Pick a location for your spooky story and use the space below to write a list of the sensations you might feel there.

Smell

Touch

Hear

See

Taste

Plan what you want to happen in each part of your spooky story here, then write it up on the following pages. Remember to use the senses from your list to create a creepy atmosphere.

Title ideas

Beginning

Build-up

Climax

Resolution

End

Questions

Is your story set in one location, or will your characters move from one place to another?

If the place is haunted, are the ghosts frightening or friendly? Or a little bit of both?

Continued...

Remember

Use your five senses to set the scene at the start of your story, but don't forget to include some action, too.

Try to show not tell how the brother and sister react to their spooky surroundings. For example, rather than saying they are frightened, show them trembling with fear.

Surprising settings

If your story moves from one location to another, setting your ghost story somewhere that's not usually spooky – such as a sunny beach – might make more impact.

Write your story title here.

Spooky words

Twilight
Crepuscular
Poltergeist
Phantom
Jinx
CURSE
Hallucination
Strange noises
Sudden death
MURDER
Shipwreck
Floating furniture
Mocking laughter
Apparition
SHADOWS
Cold chill
Unusual occurrences
Shiver
Goosebumps

26

Ending questions

Do your characters get home in the end?

If they do, use the five senses to describe how they feel to be home.

Has their adventure changed the way they feel about home?

Castaway

Here's a picture of a small group of people whose plane has crashed on a desert island. Think of a way to tell their story.

Before you write your story, plan it out on a piece of scrap paper.

You could tell the story from the point of view of one of the characters.

Or you could write as an outside observer, in the style of a newspaper report.

Story ideas

* Who are the characters in the picture? Where had they been flying to?

* Perhaps one of them has a dark secret?

* What do they do for shelter, food and water? Do they fight over who's in charge?

* Do they explore? Is there anyone – or anything – else living on the island?

* How do they signal for help? Is there a radio? Do they build a fire?

Write your story title here.

Points of view

The 'voice' you use to tell a story is known as the **narrator**.

The 'I' or 'we' point of view is called the **first person narrator**.

The **second person** tells the story from the 'you' point of view.

The **third person** tells the story from the 'he', 'she' or 'they' point of view.

You can find out more about narrative voices on page 91.

Continued...

Ways to build tension

Does a ship arrive only to turn out to be a gang of murderous pirates? Do the castaways escape or join the pirates?

Does someone build a raft and paddle off to get help?

Perhaps a tropical storm destroys their shelter and puts out the fire. What if they run out of matches?

Castaway words

Heatstroke

Makeshift fishing rod

Delirious babbling

Hunger

THIRST

Message in a bottle

Friends

ENEMIES

Ending ideas

If they are rescued, do the survivors return to their old lives or has being on the island changed them?

Do they find treasure on the island and go home millionaires?

Suspense

Fresh snowfall brings an eerie quiet to the forest, where an author of adventure stories is staying in a log cabin to write. Suddenly, the silence is broken by a clattering in the kitchen, then footsteps on the stairs. Now there are noises outside the door of the study...

Tales of the unexpected

When you keep your readers guessing about what's going to happen next, this is called suspense. Suspense keeps people turning the pages.

What next?

Here are some suggestions for building mystery and suspense as you write what happens next:

* The writer opens the door. What's out there? Is it burglars, the cat or a wild animal? There's nothing there, but a few damp footprints.

* There's a wailing noise outside. Is it someone calling for help, or just the wind in the trees?

* The writer goes to investigate...

Write your story title here.

Continued...

Useful words

Fleeing
in panic

Cold sweat

Uncertain

Apprehensive

Caught by branches

Unfamiliar

Eerie lights in the sky

Unnerving

Strange footprints
in the snow

Northern Lights

POLAR BEARS

Jumpy

Being followed?

HOWLING WOLVES

Building suspense

To build suspense, try slowing the action down at a moment of tension.

Make your character aware of every tiny detail of the forest. This could be the sound of leaves rustling or an owl hooting, or the sight of a single snowflake fluttering to the ground.

Then, speed up the action again with a sudden dramatic event.

Animal heroes

A brave animal leaps into action to rescue someone from mortal danger. Will it succeed? Is its own life under threat too?

Things to consider

* What kind of animal is your hero? Does it live in the wild, in a zoo or with a family of humans?

* Is your hero a real animal – such as a loyal pet dog?

* Or is your animal magical – like a dragon that breathes fire?

* Maybe your animal hero is rescuing other animals and the danger comes from humans?

* How does your animal move? Does it scamper, slither, scuttle, or soar?

* You could write from the animal's point of view. Can it see or hear things that humans can't?

Write your story title here.

Look it up

Finding out about the kind of animal you are writing about might give you more ideas for your story.

For example, pangolins are a kind of anteater, and they're not very intelligent. Maybe your character has a pet pangolin. It comes to rescue him or her from a gang of thugs, but almost gets distracted by a nest of ants.

Continued...

Animal words

Lolloping

Crawling

STALKING

Grunting

Squeaking

Howling

Wary

Cautious

Bristling

ALERT

Flea-ridden

FIERCE

Timid

Untamed

Slow-witted

Friendly

Hungry

Sharp-eyed

Sharp teeth

Rough tongue

Cute

Friend or foe?

A war is raging. Your hero has been parachuted behind enemy lines to join the resistance. A man and a woman take him or her to hide in a remote farm. The woman appears trustworthy, but the man seems nervous and keeps disappearing outside. What happens next?

Questions

* Is the man a double agent?

* Is your hero about to be betrayed?

* Is the man nervous because he's afraid someone will realize he's a traitor?

* Or is he worried about the woman? Maybe she's the traitor.

Body language

People often give their feelings and intentions away in their gestures. This is called body language.

There are some tips opposite on how to show whether someone is lying or very nervous. Including some of these in your story will add to the suspense.

Write your story title here.

Nervousness

Clenched fists

Fidgeting

Biting fingernails

Rubbing hands and neck

Holding tight to chair

Very quiet or babbling conversation

Lying

Lowering head

Avoiding eye contact or prolonged deliberate eye contact when speaking

Touching or scratching nose

Overly touchy/irritable

Rapid eye movement or frequent blinking

Continued...

Spy words

Shifty

Unexpected

FAKE PASSPORT

Traitor

Secret transmissions

CODED MESSAGES

Cool

Anxious

Interrogation

Sabotage

Lie detector

ALIAS

Secret identity

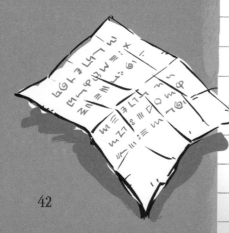

Tip

Remember to include some dialogue in your story to make the drama feel more immediate.

Perhaps your hero confronts the man to find out why he's acting so strangely.

TRACKING DEVICE
Surveillance
Darting eyes
Sweat on brow
Shaking fingers
Sudden
Mysterious
SUSPICIOUS
Watching
Disguise
HIDEOUT
Tip-off
SECRET
Rendezvous
Infiltrate
ESCAPE
Tunnel

Trapped in the desert

A group of friends is driving across the desert. All at once there is a terrible sand storm. The car engine is completely clogged and they are stranded miles from anywhere. Night falls and the baking desert turns extremely cold. What do they do?

Questions

* Does one of the friends blame another for the dangerous situation they're in?

* Does one of them get heatstroke and start acting irrationally?

* Is someone taking more than his or her fair share of water?

* What will they do if they run out of food?

* How will they survive? There are some desert survival tips on the page opposite. Try to weave them into your story.

Write your story title here.

Desert survival techniques

Shelter from the heat of the day. Travel at night when it's cold.

Without water a person will die within three days. Intake must be rationed very carefully.

A mirror used to catch the sun can be seen by possible rescuers over 100km/60 miles away.

Continued...

Desert words

Baking hot sand

GLARING SUN

Steep sand dunes

shimmering mirage

Plodding feet

Desiccated

Weary limbs

Camel train

Nomadic tribe

Oasis

Buzzing flies

Scorched

Parched

EXPOSURE

DEHYDRATION

Makeshift shelter

Sand storm

STARTING A FIRE

48

Building tension

Raising hopes and then dashing them adds to the dramatic tension.

Is that a camel train on the horizon? No, it's a mirage.

Is that the distant drone of a search plane? No, it's just a buzzing fly.

Alien landing

A flying saucer lands in a school sports field, and two blobs of slime get out. They say, "Take us to your leader" but seem unimpressed when the children take the aliens to their teacher. So they vaporize him with their ray guns.

Questions

* Do the aliens come in peace, and was vaporizing the teacher a terrible mistake?

* Or do they want to take over the world?

* Perhaps they join a class so they can find out more about life on Earth?

* How do they communicate with each other? Do they talk in strange beeps and blips? Do they use telepathy?

* What do they like to eat? Burgers? Cars? Teachers?

* Do they take the children in their spaceship to their world?

* What is it like where they live?

Write your story title here.

Alien encounters

Imagine how the aliens feel when they come across something they've never seen before. Any of these could be unfamiliar:

Someone out walking her dog. Do the aliens realize which is the pet and which is the owner?

People using their phones to take photos

Children dressed in Halloween costumes

Humans sneezing

Continued...

Alien words

Piles of ash

Laser beams

Tentacles

Eyes on stalks

Three mouths

EARTH SUITS

Medical examination

Galaxy

Nebula

Levitation

Scaly skin

Extra-terrestrial

Black hole

Alternate dimension

GOVERNMENT CONSPIRACY

Dark matter

Anti-gravity

Watch out! This ray gun vaporizes teachers.

Historical adventure

We can all travel through time – not in a fantastic time machine
that hasn't been invented yet, but in our imaginations.
Write an adventure story set in an exciting period in history.

Pick a setting

* When and where is your
  story set?

* In a medieval
  king's castle?

* At the time of the Great
  Fire of London?

* In the trenches of the
  First World War?

* In Ancient Rome,
  fighting among the
  gladiators?

* During the Ice Age,
  living with cavemen?

What if your characters
really have invented a time
machine? Will they jump
from one time to another?
How will they adjust to life
in a different era? And how
might people from the past
react to modern people
with modern gadgets?

Write your story title here.

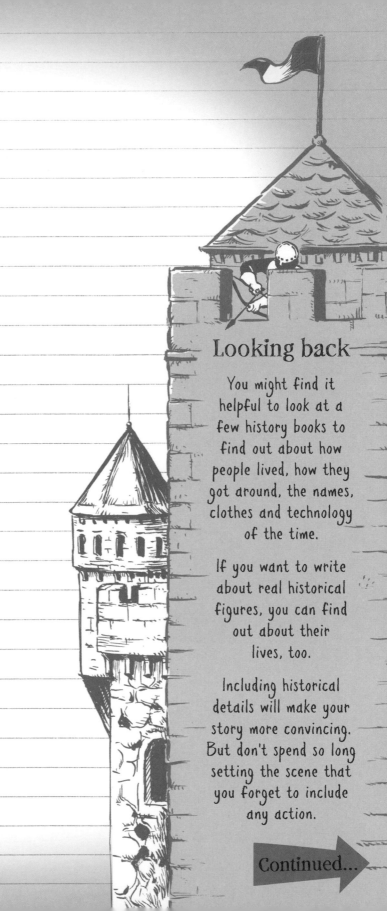

Looking back

You might find it helpful to look at a few history books to find out about how people lived, how they got around, the names, clothes and technology of the time.

If you want to write about real historical figures, you can find out about their lives, too.

Including historical details will make your story more convincing. But don't spend so long setting the scene that you forget to include any action.

Continued...

Out of time

Be careful not to include objects or slang expressions that are wrong for the time you are writing about. These are called **anachronisms**.

For example, "Chillax, Romulus. Remus is a bully but there's no need to trash his laptop," is anachronistic in an adventure set in Ancient Rome.

What's in a name?

Names go in and out of fashion, so make sure your characters' names are right for the times.

If you are writing about the First World War, use names like Harry, Albert and Ernest, rather than Kia, Shane and Wayne.

And if you were one of Cleopatra's handmaidens you'd be called Nefret or Tarset, rather than Beyoncé or Kylie.

Jungle explorers

Survey photographs reveal a magnificent lost city deep in the Amazon. A team of archaeologists heads into the jungle, but a rival bunch of treasure hunters have been bugging their calls. They do their best to get there first... contemplating sabotage, skulduggery, even murder!

This map shows some of the places your characters might see on their jungle adventure. Try to include them in your story.

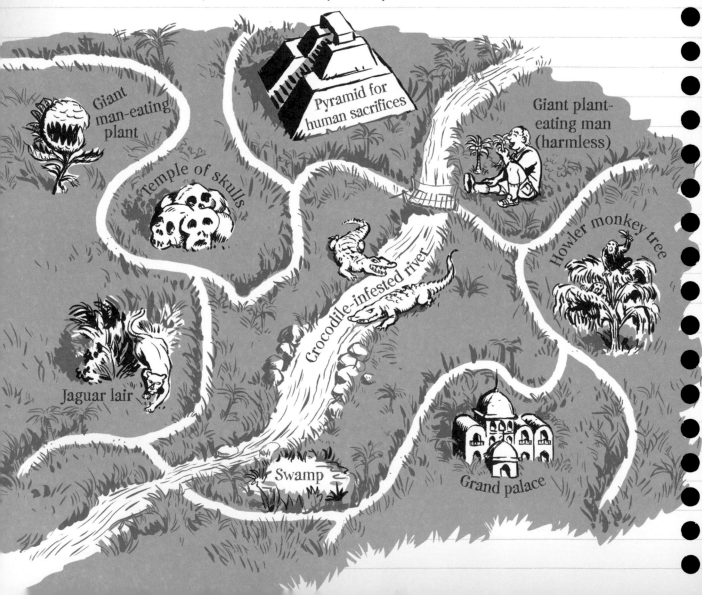

Write your story title here.

Setting the scene

Do some research to find out what the South American rainforest is like. Who lives there? How hot is it? What plants and animals might you see? How difficult is it to travel through?

Continued...

Jungle words

Waist-high grass

Spiky thorns

Leaches

Piranhas

Low throaty growl

The heavy pad
of jaguar paws

Sweltering sun

Torrential rain

Poisonous spiders

Dappled
sunlight

Impenetrable
undergrowth

SQUAWKING BIRDS

Talking parrots

Garish bright flowers

Machetes glinting
in the sunlight

Tangled vines

Steamy swamp

Suspense

Try to build up suspense in your story. Drop hints that things are going wrong. At first your characters think they are unlucky when there are accidents, or equipment breaks down. Gradually it dawns on them that someone is deliberately trying to sabotage their trip.

Continued...

Poison!

What happens if someone is poisoned by a venomous frog, but only the rival team knows where to find the antidote? Can they be trusted to help in return for a share of the treasure?

A true story

You can get lots of ideas for stories by reading about real events in newspapers. You could write up these stories and tell your own version of what happened, or you could take these events and turn them into fiction.

Getting into the action

Rather than reporting events the way they appear in the news, you could try writing in the first person, from the point of view of someone immediately involved.

Go straight into the action. For example, you could start a true story about a skydiving rescue like this:

I had never seen the ground from this high up before. It made me dizzy...

It's more exciting than:

Holly waited at the bus stop. The bus was late again. Then it started to rain. She was going to the aerodrome to do a parachute jump...

Write your story title here.

GHOSTLY HORSEMAN
spotted in quiet village

SKYDIVER'S parachute fails
Diving partner comes to rescue with seconds to spare

POLAR EXPLORER
reaches North Pole on foot

LINER SINKS
Passengers survive

PREHISTORIC BODY FOUND
DNA test proves local man is a direct descendant

Continued...

True story words

Daring rescue

PERILOUS DROP

Solo mission

Dangerous exploits

Death-defying stunt

BREATHTAKING

Astounding

Bravery

Capsize

Life-changing

Facing the elements

EXPEDITION

Exploration

WORLD RECORD

Shark attack

Your hero and a friend set off on a voyage of adventure in their dinghy. They dive into the sea for a swim, and a shark begins to circle. Suddenly they realize they have sailed into shark-infested waters...

What next?

* Can your characters get back into their boat and signal for help? How will they escape the sharks?

* What happens if night falls and your characters are left stranded?

* Are the sharks really attacking, or are they hunting for fish? Or has something happened to drive them from their usual hunting ground?

* Opposite are some tips about sharks and how to deal with them. Try to work some of these into your story.

* If your characters manage to sail away from the sharks what other surprises might they encounter on their voyage?

Write your story title here.

Shark tips

Sharks tend to hunt at dawn and dusk, and like murky water.

They are attracted by splashing, and glittering watches or necklaces.

A shark can smell blood from over a mile away – anyone who is bleeding must get out of the water as quickly as possible.

Sharks are more likely to attack a lone swimmer than a group.

Sharks can't swim backwards.

Anyone in the water should stay as still and quiet as possible – the sharks might swim away.

Eyes, gills and snout are sharks' weak spots. If they attack, hitting their snouts is the best defensive action.

Continued...

Shark words

Sensing fear

Circling fins

DARK SHADOWS

Rows of razor-sharp teeth

Dull, black eyes

Gasping for breath

Blood in the water

Noise from approaching boat

LEAPING

Rough sandpaper-skin

Macabre grin

Don't panic!

Shark attacks are very rare. You are thirty times more likely to be killed by lightning than be eaten by a shark.

Radioactive rats

A family is on a summer break on a peaceful little island, when a news flash comes on the radio. A deserted ship full of radioactive man-eating rats is drifting towards the shore...

Rats in action

* How do the rats act?

* Maybe the radioactivity has made them super smart?

* Do they have rapid conversations in squeaks and grunts?

* Do they work together or against each other?

Getting started

Try to start your story in an exciting way:

"This is an urgent news flash," came a voice from the radio. "Hah," laughed Dad. "Nothing for us to worry about, here on our safe little island!"

Rather than:

When I'm on the beach I like to lie around, go for a swim, then take a nap.

Write your story title here.

Continued...

Rat words

Scurrying

Squeaking

Frenzied horde

Glowing eyes

Green teeth

Luminous fur

SCAMPERING

Radioactive cats

FIRE TRAP

Trench

Radioactive cheese

Thick black smoke

Climbing trees

HAZARD SUITS

Zombie scientists

Evil king rat

Baited traps

Bad to worse

Just as everyone thinks they're safe, the youngest daughter goes missing. Has she been eaten by the rats? Or is she hiding somewhere out of danger?

Your story, the movie

Movie makers love adventure stories. Imagine how you would feel if one of your stories was made into a movie.

Playing parts

In movie scripts, the story is written as dialogue – sometimes with directions for the action in between.

Try writing the opening scene for a story here, in the style of a movie script.

Start a new line for each character or direction. Writing dialogue this way means you don't need speech marks.

This example shows how to write out a script.

Direction: Ali's phone rings. He answers it.

Ali: Hello. Who's calling?

Mystery agent: An ally. Your package is in the agreed place. Collect it by noon, or it will be destroyed.

Write your story title here.

Big names

Which famous actors would you choose to play the characters in your movie?

* ....
* ....
* ....
* ....
* ....
* ....

Soundtrack

Pick some songs for the soundtrack.

* ....
* ....
* ....
* ....
* ....
* ....

Story writing toolkit

Using the right words

Good writing depends on saying precisely what you mean. If a character is about to be vaporized by a death ray, don't say he's 'nervous' – say he's 'petrified'.

Write the words you think best describe how the characters feel in each of the situations below. There are some suggestions listed under the two sets of sentences.

Night is falling in the jungle, and Jack's an hour away from camp.

Jack is accosted by a hungry tiger.

Tomorrow Jack has to have a tooth taken out at the dentist's.

Anxious, frightened, terrified

Jo can't find one of her most precious comics.

Jo's brother Jack has borrowed it. Jo told him he couldn't.

It turns out, Jack hasn't borrowed it, he's sold it.

In fact he's sold Jo's entire comics collection.

Furious, enraged, angry, irritated

Good titles

Sometimes, coming up with a funny or exciting title can give you an idea for a story. A good title can also make people want to read a story too.

Sounds pretty boring...

Drizzle

Ooh, intriguing!

The Drizzle Conspiracy

THEY CAME FROM OUT OF THE DRIZZLE

Off-beat, challenging, slightly wacky. Might be worth a read???

Nothing Rhymes with Drizzle

Whoa, scary!

Here are some titles that might give you some ideas for stories.

Timmy's Hot-Air Balloon Caper

The Treasure Seeker's World Tour

The Cat that Swam the Atlantic

Trapped!

The Island of Sleep and Forgetfulness

From Clacton to Atlantis by Snail and Tricycle

Here are some story ideas. Can you come up with some exciting or funny titles for them?

Story ideas:	Possible titles:
A sea floor research station starts to flood.	
Pirates attack a luxury liner. Who will save the passengers?	
You discover a Stone-Age tribe in a remote land.	

Opening lines

Remember, it's important to hook your readers right from the start. An intriguing opening will make them want to read on, to get to the thrilling middle part and the exciting ending.

Here are three different openings for the same story:

It was an ordinary, everyday morning, but by lunchtime Emily would be fighting for her life...

The deserted bus station was a sinister place at the best of times. It was even worse in a howling gale...

"Hey Emily. It's the 13th today and you just broke a mirror in your handbag," said Sam on the morning bus. "I wonder what's going to happen for the rest of the day?"

Experiment with different openings for the same story here.

Peaks and troughs

It's easier to write a good story if you plan it carefully first. Keep your reader hooked by including lots of exciting ups and downs.

Ups and downs

Here's the outline for a thrilling intergalactic adventure with lots of ups and downs. There is space for you to add a dramatic event at point 6 and an ending at point 9.

5 They bring fresh oxygen bottles.

4 The supply crew comes aboard.

2 A new delivery is due that morning.

1 On Moon Base 12, they are running out of oxygen.

3 When it arrives, the supply ship is hit by a meteorite.

6

Planning your stories

Remember:
* Grab your reader at the start.
* Keep the middle exciting, and try not to waffle.
* End with a bang.

Don't worry about sticking rigidly to your original plot. If you have a brilliant new idea while you're writing, add it to the plan!

Endings

The ending is where you tie up any loose ends or solve any remaining problems. It should be as exciting as the rest of your story.

Ending questions

How do you think your readers would like your story to end?

With a twist or surprise?

With the hero succeeding or failing?

With the villain being defeated?

Or the mystery being solved?

Think about books you've read. How do you feel when they have sad or happy endings?

An ending should bring a story to a satisfying conclusion, but if you want to leave your readers wanting more, you could hint at another adventure to follow:

"Hooray! We saved the world again," said Tom and they all went off to have a milkshake. A pair of glowing red eyes watched them from the shadows. "Enjoy your triumph, Master Tom. You won't be so lucky next time!"

8 The supply ship has a radio so he uses that.

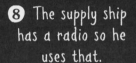

9 Plot your own ending for the Moon Base 12 story here.

7 The captain calls for help but the radio is broken.

Heroes and villains

It's important for your stories to have likeable heroes and fascinating villains. Giving your characters quirks or flaws makes them more interesting too.

Heroes

Heroes often have a remarkable strength, special skill or unusual trait that helps them succeed in their adventure.

But sometimes they can be very ordinary people. They might be reluctant heroes to start with, but in the end they triumph against the odds.

Too bad?

Don't make your villain totally bad. Maybe he or she has a soft spot for injured animals, and has a house full of them? This makes your villain intriguing and might give your story a good twist.

Below are some ideas for interesting heroes and villains. You can use the space below to add some more exciting characters that you might like to write about.

A child who was raised by woodland creatures * A caver with a bad sense of direction * An archaeologist who is allergic to dust * A pirate ship's cook who secretly feeds the rats on board his ship

*

*

*

*

*

*

*

*

*

*

*

*

*

Conjuring up locations

Remember to use all five senses when you are
describing the setting for a story. Think about what
your characters can see, hear, taste, touch and smell.

The words on the right list what you might sense in the seaside quay
pictured below. Use this page to think of one or two interesting story
settings and list the sensations you might feel there.

Hear
Squawking seagulls
Shouting sailors
Crashing waves

Taste
Ice cream
Salty sea water
Bitter lemonade

Touch
Warm breeze
Smooth pebbles
Soft sand

See
Churning tidewater
Children playing
Flapping sails

Smell
Freshly-caught fish
Oily boat fumes
Briny sea air

Exciting writing

There's more to a story than great characters, lots of action and an atmospheric setting. You need to use exciting words too. But be careful – if your readers notice the writing rather than the story, then you've overdone it.

Describing things and actions

In adventure stories, choosing good verbs (action words) can help bring the action to life. Can you add any other verbs you could use in these sentences?

He **sat** in his armchair.

... slumped ... sank

...

...

...

She **ran** to the finish line.

... raced ... sprinted

...

...

...

The rock **fell** towards us.

... plummeted ... hurtled

...

...

...

Words for things (people, animals, cliffs, ice creams...) are called nouns, and the words that describe them are called adjectives.

Words that describe verbs are called adverbs.

These make your writing more vibrant, but don't put too many in. Too much description is dull.

Adjectives   Noun   Verbs   Adjectives

The big, hairy, blond man sat sweating in the blazing-hot, sweltering sunshine, guzzling greedily on a tall, ice-cool, fizzy lemonade.

Noun   Verb   Adverb   Adjectives   Noun

It's the spice of life

Variety is important in your writing. Using very familiar phrases can make your writing sound stale. Try to think of different ways of describing these things:

A roaring fire

A howling gale

A scary monster

A towering cliff

What is it like?

As well as using adjectives to describe something, you could try comparing it with something else. For example, 'as cute as a kitten', 'as clear as crystal' or 'as cold as ice'. This kind of comparison is called a simile.

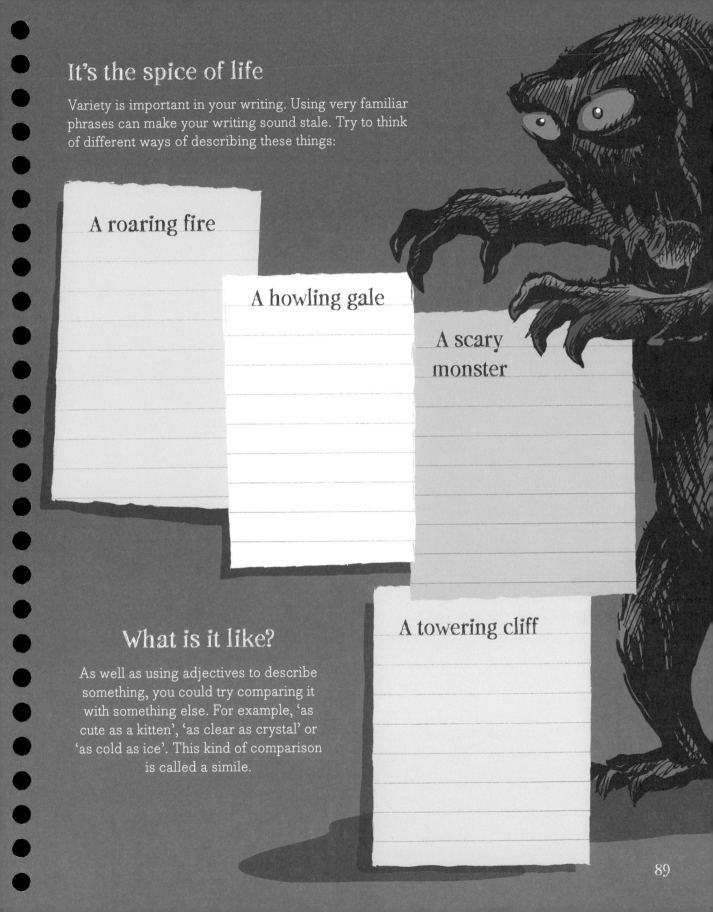

Sensational sentences

Here are some more ideas to make your stories 'unputdownable'. Even if you read a lot, you might not notice the writer using these techniques. But these little touches make a story more readable.

Short and snappy

At times of great tension, use a few short sentences.

So this was it. He'd tried and failed. He was going to die.

(Don't overdo it, though.)

Slow it down

Try slowing down the action as your story reaches its climax. Put in tiny details as your character faces his or her biggest ever challenge. What is he thinking? What does she see? Does an unsolved mystery suddenly make sense?

Add a paragraph to the dramatic passage below. Raise the tension with a few snappy sentences, then slow things down.

Standing on the deck of her yacht watching the sunset Yasmin felt her boyfriend's arm around her waist. It felt wet and slimy. She looked down. It was the tentacle of a giant octopus...

Which tense works best?

Try using different tenses to see which suits your story best. Most writers use the past tense.

> We came into the hall. There were a couple of jaguars prowling around. They looked hungry and they snarled as they saw us.

But using the present tense, as though the action is happening as you write, can be exciting. Be careful, though – reading a whole story like this can be exhausting.

> We come into the hall. There are a couple of jaguars prowling around. They look hungry and they snarl as they see us.

Stick with it

It's important to be consistent in your writing style, otherwise your story can become confusing to read. Make sure you stick with whichever tense you decide to use.

Narrative voices

As well as experimenting with different tenses, you could also try different points of view.

First person

(I or we) This point of view is good for adventure stories because the character telling the story is directly involved in the action.

> "I will never forget the moment we came into the hall," said Grandma. "There were a couple of jaguars prowling around and they were obviously hungry. They caught sight of me and snarled, and I thought my last moments had come."

Third person

(He, she or they) This is useful if you want to show your story from different angles.

> "Now, stand against that wall so I can zap you," said Doctor Dogbreath. Agent X looked up at the night sky. Unseen, in the shadows lurked a third figure...

Second person

(You) This is an unusual choice, but it can be a good way to bring your readers right into the story.

> You abseil down the mountain, desperate to get back to base before nightfall. To your horror you come upon the frayed end of a rope...

Very short stories

See if you can write a whole story – with a beginning, middle and end – on these little scraps of paper here. Get your imagination racing, and remember, there's so little space every word has to count.

A stuntman is making a parachute jump. When he pulls the parachute release, it breaks off in his hand…

A deep-sea diver is investigating a shipwreck, when a swordfish appears out of nowhere and slices through her air hose…

You discover a tribe of ape-like creatures deep in the forest. They announce they are going to cook you for dinner…

Micro fiction

Can you write a story in under 140 characters?
(That's letters, spaces and punctuation marks.)
Here are a couple to show how it can be done:

Celia was addicted to blogging on her phone. Then, one icy morning, her thumbs froze, locking firm onto the keypad. Her final post: Hel...

Joe's best friend was his pet python Penelope. He bought her a dead rat to eat on her birthday. Unfortunately she ate him instead.

Now use the grid below to write your own micro story. It has been divided into 140 squares so you can see how many characters you are using.
(Tip: You might want to try this in pencil first, in case you go over the limit.)

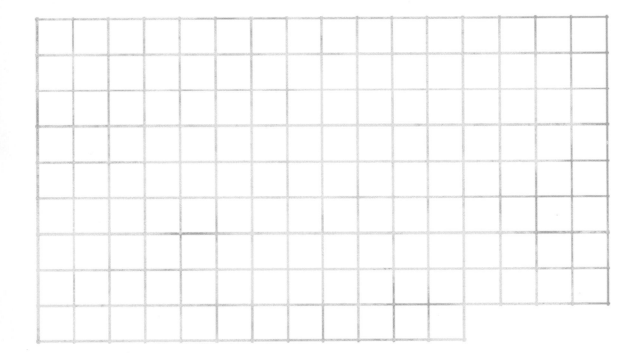

Even more tips

Great writing needs some skill as well lots of brilliant ideas. Here are some more tips to help you make your writing as readable as possible.

Boring but important

Make your spelling and punctuation as good as you can. Mistakes can draw your readers' attention to YOU the writer, and away from the story. It's also a good idea to avoid using too much slang or text speak.

Which of these two passages do you find more readable?

Say yor prayerz punk this is the Last time yull evr interfere With my plans 4 world Dominashon sed dr horribul pntng his hairpon at my <3.

"Say your prayers, punk. This is the last time you'll ever interfere with my plans for world domination," said Dr. Horrible, pointing his harpoon at my heart.

Clichés

When you use an expression that's *too* familiar this is called a cliché. Clichés can make writing sound stale. See if you can rewrite these passages to make them sound fresher:

I took my eye off the ball and lost the game. The winning team was over the moon.

Time will tell whether we manage to save them in the nick of time.

(Tip: This sentence also repeats a word, which is bad style.)

Finding inspiration

If you ever get stuck for ideas,
don't panic. Why not try one of these:

Turn an event from real life into a story.

Imagine what would happen if characters from
different books or movies met each other.

Use one of your dreams, or nightmares, as the starting
point for a story.

Write a sequel to a book you've enjoyed.

Catch the moment

Many writers keep a journal or
notebook handy so they can catch
their ideas before they forget them.

You never know when inspiration
for a story might strike. So if you
hear an curious phrase or a funny
joke, or come up with a mind-
blowing idea, jot it down.

Let's hear it!

Read your story aloud. You'll really
notice where it drags – much more than
you would if you just read it in your mind.

Which words are getting in the way?

What can you get rid of?

Have you repeated descriptive words?
Think of other words you can use.

If you read your story aloud and it
still sounds really exciting, then it
almost certainly is!

Top tips for terrific writing

Remember to show not tell. It will really bring your writing alive.

Use all five senses, if you can. This will take readers right into your story.

Use words with precision. If you mean 'ravenous' don't say 'slightly hungry'.

And finally… Think about every word and sentence. Make sure your reader
is always desperate to find out what happens next!

Acknowledgements

Story starters and tips written by Paul Dowswell

Illustrated by Paul Hoppe

Edited by Ruth Brocklehurst

Designed by Laura Wood and Ian McNee

Quicklinks

For links to websites where you can find more tips and inspiration for
writing amazing adventure stories, go to www.usborne.com/quicklinks
and type in the title of this book. Please read our internet safety
guidelines at the Usborne Quicklinks website